SOUTH EASTERN STAGES

ALSO BY ANTHONY KELLMAN

Poetry
In Depths of Burning Lights (1982)
The Broken Sun (1984)
Watercourse (1990)
The Long Gap (1996)
Wings of a Stranger (2000)
Limestone (2008)

Fiction
The Coral Rooms (1994)
The Houses of Alphonso (2004)

Edited
Crossing Water (1992)

ANTHONY KELLMAN

SOUTH EASTERN STAGES

PEEPAL TREE

First published in Great Britain in 2012
Peepal Tree Press Ltd
17 King's Avenue
Leeds LS6 1QS
UK

ISBN 13: 9781845231989

ACKNOWLEDGEMENTS

I express gratitude to the editors of the following magazines in which some of these poems, in slightly different form, first appeared:

Bim (Barbados) for "Nature as Shrink", and "The Henrietta Marie"; *Colere* (Iowa) for "Travellers"; *Journal of Post-Colonial Writing* (Oxford) for "The Bleaching Process" and "The Masters, Part Two"; *New Delta Review* (Louisiana) for "Tale of the Yard Fowls"; *The Polyglot* (Georgia) for "Happy Among People" and "Tuk Haikus"; *Visions International* (Texas) for "The Migration"; *Wasafiri* (London) for "Three Beaches", "Every Carolina", "The Room", "Paraplegic Diver", "The Old Bell Ringer", "Caliban" and "After the Rain, Part Two"; "The Old Bell Ringer" and "Caliban" appears in the anthology, *Beyond Sangre Grande: Caribbean Writing Today,* Ed. Cyril Dabydeen. Toronto: TSAR Publications, 2011.

CONTENTS

THE OLD BELL RINGER
For Lawrence Pilgrim

I catch a glimpse of him in the foyer, seated
on an old folding chair. Dark shades,
patterned tan shirt, mousse-brown pants.
He's waiting to perform a
thirty-six-year old calling,
patient there with his mat of white hair.
He's never missed a single ringing,
not at six; not at twelve; not at six.

The arched entrance, like an aureole, holds him
bottom right, as in a photo, where he dozes
still as a portrait, becoming part of the chair,
blending into the green louvred door
set in the coral stone walls.

The capacious main building
encircles him in its arms.
Its triptych of windows
in arched stained glass echoes the
light and colour he brings.

He rode his old Raleigh bike
from Bayville through the morning's
dull screen of rain which is falling still,
though it's thinning now and more pellucid.
Will he pre-empt the ringing at noon,
ride home before it pours again?

He rises precisely at noon,
a blue baseball cap on his head
– as if he wasn't dozing at all –
with the alacrity of a man half his age.
Flicking the rope from its bolts

9

on the coral wall, he coaxes language
from the hundred and seventy-year-old bell,
eighteen syllables in a 3-3-3-9 measure.

The world listens and responds:
all the meditating faithful,
all those city workers checking
and setting their watches by his time.

HAPPY AMONG PEOPLE

The slow easy walk to lucid, moss-less aquamarine;
the towel with enclosed car keys
laid on a low sea grape;
the waterline twenty feet away.
"When I come I bring my aloes, you know;
'tis dread this summer, boy." A teen to his mate.
A woman stares, not at me
but at a spot next to me. Quick side-glance
reveals a yellow orb bobbing
on the tide – the orange which escaped
my pocket when I nose-dived in.
I grab and playfully toss and re-catch it.
"You want piece?" I ask.
"Yeah. Sure." So we soak our portions
in mutual salt.

Behind me, a man ducks his girlfriend
who's much taller than he.
She pleads for him to stop. Since he persists,
she does something that
bends him in two, makes him walk
slowly and painfully to shore.
"Boy, she hit me de place which gives
de most pleasure and de most pain,"
he says as he passes by me.
"A rematch?" I ask,
and the nearby spectators laugh.

At the water's edge, a young woman
in a black one-piece
acclimatises her months-old child
to the sea's touch. Mother squats
on one knee in the shallows,
baby on the other raised for a table-top.

11

Now and then she scoops handfuls
of water and bathes the little one
who takes it all without resistance.
I imagine a painter capturing this:
sea birds racing overhead; casuarinas waving in the background;
the mother gently initiating the smooth-skinned child;
a foreground of rippling aquamarine.

Somewhat recovered, our man
rises with a huge ball of sand,
hefts and throws it from hand to hand,
trying to taunt her. "I coming fo' you."
"Come nuh. I in deep water, yuh know."
"Nuh problem. I can swim with it in one hand."
He wades more purposefully toward her,
releases a perfectly thrown sand ball.
She cries out, chases him. Everyone's laughing.
The lovers gain shore, flop down on the sand, rolling
around 'til they're both fully covered
with a sand shield...

As I leave, they're re-entering the water
to rinse. The watermark is less
than a foot from the sea grape
where I left the towel.

PARAPLEGIC DIVER

After a punctilious suiting-up
by the leader, he was thrown into the sea
one mile out. A smile rode his face
in his curled foetal descent,
the mid-morning sun lambent
on the water.

He was the first to feel gravity's assault,
made the neutralizing configurations
as pressure increased:
weight-belt adjustment, swallowing, nasal control.
Soon, he settled in the neutral space of the sea.

He'd, no doubt, done this many times
before, and on this particular vacation,
with these particular people, for no one gasped,
stared, or eyed the leader – except me.

One by one we followed him,
found polyphony in the common salt
of arcane gills, coral crenellations,
monarchical turtles.
The limitless depths issued out beyond us.
Our leader kept closest to him,
turning him at different angles when he signalled.

An hour later, back on deck,
I spoke to him. An attorney.
Still practising? Still practising.
Now he looked so much younger,
face burnished gold,
flushed with the rush of the dive,
eyes creased at the corners in ripples
and bright as starfish.

THE MIGRATION
(In Tuk Verse, Movement #2)

Why did we leave? And what did we know
finning below reefs, in our once-sure
sheltering place? Who called from Trinidad,
forced a betrayal of country? Was
leaving certain for uncertain, changing from
lime to clay and siltstone,
folly? A desire to carve an option?
Is the only true exile a forced one?
We chose to leave, to abandon coral,
because (so you say) it looked to us dull,
like a faded fan, an old worn jacket.
Was it spite prodded by a lip cut
by some apparent wrong?
We needed a surer feeding ground.
We left in order to remain,
ours the face of Silver Men
who made a history
built from pounding steel.
Ours the face of other shoals
heading to various points north,
leaving sacred sand, the familiar ground
that references one's shape and sound.
Yet, sooner or later, in some shape,
our homing input will be made.
Social security and pension cheques
multiply with exchange rates
from careers made across the sea,
not as much by choice, as by necessity.

THE HENRIETTA MARIE

In the new age of Commerce and Reason,
mist rises from loud dissolute ports
in London, Bristol, Liverpool, the mist
of dreams, hesitant and hopeful,
and the feral certainty of desire.
John Taylor, part owner of cargo and vessel, pulls
quill tip from an inkwell, writes and witnesses his will,
wonders the connection between property and death.

Kneller, too, wonders, his raised brush bird-pecking
the palette for an outline lasting 'til New Elmina.
There, his dour subject had glimpsed the Congo's
wondrously woven raffia textiles in a rainbow of dyes,
yet remained oblivious to Benin's scholastic height.
Endemic misery seethes in oils.

For the weary, low-paid crew, clutched by past failures,
grown as hardened as their captain to human misery,
the only canvas is on the masts.
Some escaped the newfangled craze for gin,
the lanes where suicides kept rising,
heartlands of neglect, where trade tools
and cooking pots were sold to satisfy "the habit".

By mid crossing, half the crew
and untold slaves are gone –
officers, carpenters, apprentice, cook,
gunner and mate, cooper and mate.
The sharks gnawed them as they'd eaten rats
to stay alive a little longer. At New Calabar,
Taylor had begun his journey towards death.
He remembers Barbados three years earlier,
the pounds of profit, Shuller's
anxious hands examining two hundred slaves,

but is too sick to see this cargo of humans
exchanged in Port Royal for a full load:
hogsheads of sugar, cotton and ginger.

The storm is sudden,
sudden the sinking feeling of the end
of days as the hull strikes reef and pewter basins,
bottles and plates scatter like human parts.
The strewn ivory brought from New Calabar
won't find translation in music.
Coins like fish scales sink to the depths
with the slow delicate turns of dancers.

THREE BEACHES

1

Saltiest of all, the most panoramic:
the port's three sugar loaders labour
in a sucrose landscape sloping upward and inward,
like a crew cut, to the cane fields' anemones,
their waving lamentations.
My people should come first, not European quotas.
Why should my blood have to settle
for lumpy Guatemalan sugar in their tea?
Choppy today. The sizzle and splash mingles
with a tragic drone, (in intent, as ancient
as the world's oldest profession), as tower cranes
lower cement-mix that, encircling vertical steel,
will soon become the walls of a rebuilt hotel.
Imploded five years ago, its determination
never diminished. It took that long
for its ashes to come alive again,
bigger but younger, thicker but stronger,
like the intruder in "Philip, My Dear",
the male stranger who stole into the Palace,
past all that high-tech security,
through all those empty rooms,
to the Queen's bedroom.

2

Seabirds foray between the silently snorting
rum refinery towers and the port whose southern
waterfront's packed with limestone boulders
tight as the dry-stone walls of North Yorkshire.
Behind these, freighters off-load grain.
Some of it spills onto the adjacent highway
when the trucks take off. The birds here glow in health,
genesis of the neighbourhood's name – Birds River.
The river's gone, its angling broken by the highway, housing
development, progress. The birds remain,
stitching the air over aquamarine sea
and the ribboning sand where a man sets up
a plywood wicket and bowls to his young son,
nourishing his craft from early, like the father
of the Williams sisters. Here, a jogger
can put in two miles each way.
The jealous water calls, and it's wrong not to
respond. Least salty, just right for the orange
hefting in the swim-trunk's pocket, another ball
whose juice fires vitamin C with a stream
of salt water down the throat.
The highway's traffic is no distraction, no match
for the vivid lace of sea grapes spreading over the shore's
upper fringe of sand or for the sheltered
settled tub of one's peace.

3

Most private of all, cut off from traffic
and the world beyond, its hugging arc
the orchestra's quarter circle;
its roof the foliage of high-rising manchineel,
its seating low sea grape, exclaiming sisal.
Royal palms, fronds clustered, flutter like pom poms.
The golden palms' gold-dusted arms curve
from the ground up, pulse like the feathers
of some exotic bird. The sea voices its bold
choral harmony, waves cresting and racing to shore,
conducting a diminuendo of human voices.
Those heard resurrect the ancient codes:
you greet, you smile, you ask how-d'you-do.
The person whom you pass and almost touch
on this intimate sand could be a god
whose voice mingles with water
on the shore of dreams.

NATURE AS SHRINK

The room is open air
with walls of manchineel, sandbox, sea grape,
glazed with epic sunlight and the sea's
choral voicings. An orange-coloured lifeguard station
in case things get outta hand. Come, nuh!
Sit and see on the couch of sea and sand.

An old wizened fellow wearing a poplin cap
speaks to the soft ripples.
A woman fills plastic bottles with saltwater
for laxative use later on and sings with the surf.
A child, yellow arm-floats replacing human arms,
is less irritable after this cooling.
Two women peel and break sacramental grapefruits.
They laugh and shout, "Ou! Ouuuu!"
The curled rinds bob on the tide like
orange paper boats or arm-floats gone adrift.

The saltwater bottles leave. A man enters.
At once, he speaks to the wind
of surviving lost employment, the urgency
and grief in his voice no less intense
than Iona Potapov's two centuries earlier
in the Russian cold who learnt, the hard way,
nature's ears are kinder than men's.

SUNBLOCK

While others apply time-release,
vitamin-laced lotion with its UV sunscreen,
or nothing at all, he lathers his arms and legs
with ordinary sand until only a small window
in the centre of his back is left open.
To complete the ritual, he lies, face-up, on the sand,
and swishes from side to side.
Such movements seem spastic
to the uninformed. He gets strange looks.
Now fully lathered, he sits upright,
scans the beach with a hyphenating grin,
then rises for the last rite, the unctuous swim.
Grains fall off him like bread crumbs.

TUK HAIKUS
(in Tuk Verse, Movement #1)

1

Crosby, Clooney, Kaye and
Ellen, with one heart,
sing and yearn for the snow. A black

hand with spotless silver
shaker from which rains
frothing cocktails. A hand. No face.

2

Tadpoles, active, white and
sailing at high cost,
dot the southern Miami coast.

3

Round a screen of bushes,
blithely as four sheep,
workmen wetting the grass in peace.

4

Tails of light and sand-arcs
dune-ing the sea bed.
Silver severed cavali's head.

5

Scowl of clouds on northeast
sky and the southwest
sand made brighter, like flame, by this.

6

Lights are stitching joy that
spirals up their legs:
royal palms that all wink Noel.

MANGO TREE

Each day, in harmony with the black birds'
light rapid tweets and late June winds
that turn the paling to a fence of castanets,
my mango tree faithfully drops one ripe fruit,
some time between six and eight o'clock.

I hear its personal thud
and muted roll on the grass outside the door.
I receive and wash it good,
the juicy pith submitting to my want,
my direst need.

That's why I always leave the door open
to let the freshness sweep through:
those co-operative winds which, each day,
release such fine fruit
to complete my breakfast table.

AFTER THE RAIN (PART TWO)
(in Tuk Verse, Movement #1)

A shore that shimmers brown,
in health, fecund,
after showers that purged for days.

Saw, like writhing surf, small
fishes with their gold
tresses laced with the whitest meld.

Pregnant woman enters
water with a child.
Golden fingers. Capacious smile.

The fronds of palms all hail,
like snappers' gills,
soughing umbrage, our greenest days.

CALIBAN

(Tuk Verse, Movement #3)

Walt Whitman wrote that something
startled him where he thought he
was safest. Across the sea,
restless in the castle of his skin,

Lamming knew that feeling too,
the need to flee the class war
between school and home, withdraw
to the dream of England's widening view;

the ports that hailed colonial
children, the beckoning cities
with more than the old simplicities,
once loved but now provincial.

He fled, leaving behind the one class
he loved for exile's chilly pleasure,
the indifference of Northern mother.
But like searching light through glass

his words reached back to us. To what?
An island that doesn't feel it needs
its authors, that by their size reads
worth in salaries and house-plot;

that tattled him with mockery:
'In England, he'd spend each hour
on fast sports cars, women, wouldn't sponsor
the West Indian students with free

lectures, readings.' Did they ever buy
one of his books, or just rice him?
Leave the vile ad-hominem
to stiff-suits. Critics need to try

for richness and the word-crafter's
pith. Stiff-suits know only a folkish kitsch.
But now, nestling near a cricket pitch
like a giant crane, our living master

watches young Bayville boys bat and bowl –
like Sobers? Good! Lamming's home,
living here, no more to roam,
no more the long gap, restored to coral.

TALE OF THE YARD FOWLS
(in Tuk Verse, Movement #2)

A monarchical cock resumes its strut
circled by several Pertilotes,
his adventurings as legendary
as a hip-swinging Bob Marley's,
though to control the population
swell he's been practising onanism.
Faithfully adopting Anancy's tricks,
he can change supernal plumes in minutes.
One's the face of a college professor
known for pretences of immense ardour,
despite auguries of scary hair-
loss and a hermit crab's crooked frame,
who still persists along iniquitous paths,
too-wicked-to-be-droll, so-transparent-as-to-be-sad.
Another's the face of the culture manager,
adept at granting special favours
for devotion to cynical backyard
deals, compliance to playing the toad,
that boost the crenellated heft
of a turgid ego, give it a sweet uplift.
I made him, brags the old writer;
'twas my suggestions made him brighter.
These fowls will try to take you out
should you refuse loyalty to that pecking spot.
There's no return…
you're thought of as someone who is dead…

HISTORY OF A COMMODE

It entered the home modestly,
a merchant family's gift to their chauffeur,
its four-knobbed base heavy with mahogany,
the lid and cover of pine.
It predated the caned kind with the comfy
armrests by fifty years.

Over thirty years after the chauffeur
and wife passed, the children
all on their own, it was still there,
covered with cotton cloth in a storage room.
One child, in the States,
determined to keep the family home,
rented it out, minus that one room.
Besides the commode, you would have found
(also in mahogany, once the poor man's furniture)
a triptych glassware cabinet; caned rocking,
upright and Morris chairs – the last
donated to The School For the Blind.
The thin, wiry supervisor had told him
they'd repair the jangled or broken legs,
re-cane, auction, deduct repair costs,
give him the difference. Back in the States
he'd called twice each year for three years
to a "We ain' auction them yet" refrain.

The fifth year he returns, gives the Morris chairs
to The School as a gift to avoid the wasted
long-distance calls, the stress.
Yet, he can't help thinking the wiry
supervisor woman's making a small fortune
this way. Perhaps, he should give her
the commode. A nice idea for revenge,
but a battle he could do without.

He thinks, *I have no use for the commode.*
It takes up valuable space in the room.
It must go. Fleetingly, he thinks
of just putting it on the roadside
for the Sanitation Authority to collect.
Shame runs hotly, coldly, under his skin,
as if he's violated something ancestral,
some deep loyalty to his past.

One windy cerulean day, he loads
it in the back of the hired car, sets out to sell.
Hastings. An old weather-beaten Great House
owned by a grandson of the merchant Tempro.
The grandson is emaciated, stringy, dusty
but personable, friendly. He waits.
From the trellised porch he sees through
the wooden door louvres, hills of furniture,
dust-coated, arranged in no particular order.
Tempro couldn't take it. Would be too hard to sell.

On the West Coast swollen with its umbrage
of tropical trees (frangipani, palms, ackees, mangoes,
mahogany, coconut, breadfruit,) he stops
at La Galerie Antique, a well-stocked
place with a Black proprietress whose indifference
indicates she feels him incapable of purchase.
He states his purpose. Impatiently,
irritably, she dismisses and ignores him.
A moke, parked in the driveway, blocks his exit.
"I need to get out of here! Whose car is this!!"
The blonde driver promptly responds, lets him out.
The proprietress stares with contempt.

Further along the West Coast
to Antiquaria 11, a more intimate space
with collectables as well,

one, a five-inch black and white TV.
The Black attendant's talkative,
though not in the prating sense.
Our man's drawn to a copper mariner's
telescope over two centuries old,
surprisingly leaden, that'd extend a sailor's
or pirate's eye for miles on the ocean's face.

The voluble attendant suggests another place
"Up the hill". Greenwich House Antiques.
He's tired, doubtful now. She suggests
using it as a side table, the inside for storage.
He'd love to but just don't have the space.
When she mentions the Museum, he fills
with excitement, thinks, *I can contribute*
to our heritage, preserve it for posterity.

The Museum would take it only if they had none
or if any they had was younger than his.
The woman at the desk converses with
the furniture curator. He'll check the stock.
"Get back to me tomorrow."

Next day, after laundry at "Fresh N' Clean",
he heads to The Museum.
He'd been tempted to dump the commode,
tired of having to chauffeur it around
as though it were some visiting royalty,
the rear passenger seat lain flat, taking up valuable space,
an unwanted companion a whole week now.
The curator, a large young man
with trenchant eyes, said, "Had you brought
it in a year ago, we'd have taken it at once.
We have three of them now, but let me talk
to the Director. Call me on Monday."
On Friday, prematurely, he returns, itching for release,

31

some decision at least. The curator says,
"Good to see you. Bring the commode on Monday.
We'll take it."

So this human necessity, after days
transported over asphalt or dirt tracks
leading to Great Houses,
after centuries loyally serving masters' arses,
finds at last a dignified resting place for future
generations to view. It's the oldest of its kind.
He hears his now inculpable heart beat slower,
glad he hadn't dumped it for collection,
but wonders how many other artefacts,
laden with time's mahogany age-rings,
may have been lost this way,
placed for disposal on history's curb.

THE ROOM

He had his little place tidy
and neat as his late mother's herb garden.
White and black milk crates stacked
in vertical pairs, they contained
so much of his life: boom box;
work shoes, polish, brush; books,
mailing envelopes, glue, paper clips;
a coin container. The stationery tier
was capped with hardboard, wrapped
in black and white vinyl, wired tight
to the top crate – his little table where he ate
oak flakes with eggs fried on a hotplate
which rode the third pair of crates. In that tower:
olive oil, canned soups, beans, tuna. And,
under those, like mundane afterthoughts
in a herb garden, tennis shoes, bottled water.

The one room separated like two thoughts:
one side held an iron bed, chest of drawers,
and his experimental crated kitchen;
the other, a toilet, basin, and shower.
Again, inventing, splitting thoughts,
he turned the face basin into a kitchen sink
separating it from toilet and bath
with a beige cotton curtain with a pattern
of little blue and wine-coloured miniature
houses. He'd wash his hands
under the shower faucet instead.

Invasions of roaches teased
further ingenuity. To keep the pests
off toothbrush and shaver, he suspended
these from the bath ceiling on a wire
toilet set where they remained
like silent chimes or witnesses.

Although doing better with roaches in winter,
he could never fully exterminate them.
Each time he left for the big city,
he faithfully sprayed Ortho Home Defense
in corners, around the range, fridge, the one door.
Those whom he shot directly, kicked briefly, then grew taciturn.
Luckier ones crept into holes and trenches
like battle-weary but determined soldiers –
until on his return the fresh odour of food drew
them out again. He couldn't win.
Although the Ortho said "Good for indoor
and outdoor use", he worried about fumes
locked so tightly in his room.
So he kept one window cracked, as advised
each year against carbon monoxide poisoning:
safe, alone, protected, organised.

EPIPHANY THROUGH A SMALL TOWN

…A garbage can brimming with last week's leavings.
A Baptist graveyard with fresh-cupped flowers.
A canal full with recent rain. Glazed
with indifference, a pertly flowering magnolia.
Past the dollar store and small-town Farmer's Bank,
a family of six approach the bus; one,
a Nike-clad youth, baseball cap on backwards, headphones
clasping his head, hitches baggy jeans drooping below white boxers.
Two of the women break ranks, hug and kiss
the arrivants, then wait in waving merriment
in the Tyre Center lot. PRAISE HIM shouts
from the front of a cerulean T-shirt.
In the distance, a phalanx of forty-foot pines.
Woodstacks. Sunlight over a meadow, green from
last week's rain. Sweet sunlight over pasturing cows.
Silent black cows. Sweet silent sunlight.
Land For Sale. Five to Fifty Acre Lots.
Baby pine groves delicate and fragile as life.
Whenever we manage to become intimate, you spoil it.
You get authoritarian, as if you own me. It was…
it was so long ago I forget when we last made love.
I don't think we'll ever make love again.
It's best this way, to live conveniently — Someone mows the lawn,
pays the bills, takes out the garbage. Someone cooks, washes,
buys groceries. Fine. As if summoned, rain clouds
close in like an overpass. Then, as suddenly, light
softens on adult pines. Storage For Rent.
Baby pines stretch for miles like rows of rattooned
sugar cane, the hard mauve stalks waving,
sweet in maturation, but calloused
and burdened within each self-protecting carapace.

TRAVELLERS

They prod and clutch belongings in lines
of races, languages, cultures, classes,
bound for Houston, New York, Philly,
San Antonio, Miami, Mobile,
Tennessee, Lake Charles, Baton Rouge,
New Orlean's gothic and its jazz.
Small children cry, restless –
not from hunger since they've been snacking
all this time – just tired, irritable.
Parents scowl at bus staff.
The 7.30 a.m. leaves at 7.15,
a transport that's normally forty minutes late.
The next bus leaves at 11.00 a.m.,
then news, through rattling speakers:
this one has been delayed.

From where do they come? Where are they going?
An Indian youth sits on her Pullman,
legs delicately crossed, right hand
propping a concentrated mind.
Young men, in the headphones' grip,
possess an enviable distraction
from those with nothing to do but shift and sigh.
A Latino lays two suitcases down,
sits on the terminal floor, kicks
off shoes, reclines on the baggage.
You can hear relief from the smile on his face.
A teenager wears "Gangster" on a T-shirt
that is matted with sequins.

Faces of resilience. Patient faces.
It's pointless to lodge complaints here.
Reinforcements will promptly be summoned.
You'll be escorted outside.

Hours and hours of delay do not mean
a lunch voucher; only more waiting (or you
know what you can do…)

Many have no car, no license;
others had theirs taken for DUIs;
some have nightmares of planes
diving into towers; others
bear some disabling handicap.
And there are those who need
this particular solitude.
In a community of strangers they can
hear their own blood. Conserving
energy, they can concentrate on purposes,
their hearts' destinations.

REFRESHING

After the evacuation notice on the station lot
where people parked for free, after
the tip-off last week of an adjacent
public sliver of space, my returning bus
slides into Lane 5. At once, I look to that wedge,
and my anxiety rises higher.
A green tarp strapped across the rear windshield
to the bumper and hubcaps makes the
Japanese car glow like a firefly.
Someone smashed the window to get the stereo.
But what thief would go to the trouble
of fitting tarpaulin over shattered glass?
I'm to be towed then. New city regulations
prohibit public access to that lot-slice,
free to motorists until three days ago.

I approach like a cat unsure its mouse is alive.
Setting down my bags, I peer under the tarp
at the shattered window, at the glass splinters
splayed all over the back seat.
"Some workmen in the lot behind the fence
were mowing." I spin around to the porter standing
over me calm as a pointed gun. "Sent a rock over the fence.
Tried to slip away, but I told them who you were;
that you'd be back today. I look out for the car for you."
I proffer ten dollars, thank him.
He looks thirtyish, has a lined moustache
and his six feet of cool could be mistaken for shyness.
"They left information on how to get in touch."
I look into the car again. On the back seat,
an edge of paper juts from under a piece of glass.

Slowly exiting the station, I make the call.
Wind pours freshly through the rear

window space onto the back of my head.
I received a rental car on Monday.
On Wednesday, their Specialist Unit
came to the hotel and installed the new windshield.
Refreshing.

RECYCLED

Across the ceiling, curtains hung canopy-style
to make his one room on North Avenue artsy.
He'd lived there four years; another four at Heard.
When finally he moved to the big city
and didn't need them any more, he gave them
to his new neighbour who was having a yard sale.
He helped her put heavier things out
on the front lawn which sloped gently down
to the ivy-clothed guard wall of her 20's Craftsman.
One of those things was a red Persian rug.
He rolled it out on the fescue, dogwood
shadows fluttering on the surface.
There were two threadbare spots the size of his palms.
Apart from these, the rug could have been new.
A middle-aged brunette with softly bevelled features
climbed the driveway and headed straight for it.

    "Don't sell it for two hundred," she said
in a softly bristling tone.

    "Can't afford to get it repaired."

    "No, no. It'd only cost four hundred to repair…
Use those curtains over there for temporary pads
'til you can get it fixed…" He watched and smiled
as she reached for the old drapes.

    "…But that is a great rug you have there.
Cost thousands new. Hold on to it."
The old hangings, spotted with miniature
wine-roofed houses, would function again,
though in a somewhat different role,
a hundred and fifty miles from where
they were first conceived.

THE MASTERS
(Part Two)

There's something in the air
between carefully arranged silverware,
between khaki pants, navy blazers,
formal dresses, and heels stepping in sync
on the parquet floor, between
lanes of azalea and foaming dogwood,
something whispering "I'm losing",
the last words of one who felt wealth
and influence could earn death's immunity.
Ghosts of long-dead golfers waltz between
32 types of roses, 800 plants,
then strike famous poses.

It's a Victorian sense of manners,
a Victorian fear of scandal.
To be polite at all costs. Never to offend,
or appear to, a repression of emotion
which is the repression of truth,
Freud's root of all mania, an inherited wound
thumb-printed through life in Hootie Johnson's
 "…[N]ot at the point of a bayonet."

Authors' clubs, women's clubs,
and community foundations
clutch, cling, and cleave to ancient civilities:
from reading only "regional" literature
to men gathering in barber shops to watch hair cut
to never double-dipping a vegetable bite,
to scowling at couples of different races.

Many Black Americans shrug
and run the same parochial gauntlet.
Six ninth-graders with empty hands

made Rosa T. Beard start the Debutante Club.
Etiquette. Manners. Tradition. Fear of scandal.
Jaws tightly set against the interracial date.

Sunday mornings it's "us and we
and they and them; and even they
and them from other worlds who look like us" –
those who've come, dreams no longer postponed
and other once-embraced worlds forgotten.

Landscape, warmed
with gardenia's magical scent
and wisteria's bee-humming bliss,
cups a cold stare, a forgotten bondage;
the venial fault roars and sets in,
fearful to welcome the immigrant,
unable to shake that hand.

BILTMORE

Perhaps he felt compelled
to actualize the pun in his name.
Three floors on eight thousand blue-ridged acres,
thirty-three beds, forty-three baths, sixty-five fireplaces.
Two hundred and fifty rooms.
Imagine the critical groans
at the start of construction
near the end of a century,
twenty-six years after the war
that left so many with so little –
the penalty for that excess:
his untimely death and Cornelia's marriage
to a stranger who inherited his wealth.

Let's call a castle a castle.
A winter garden, a billiard room, a banquet hall,
an organ loft, a breakfast room tinkling
with Minton and Baccarat china;
walls adorned with embossed Spanish leather,
Italian red marble, the fireplace framed
with jasperware tiles, family portraits hanging
as if the subjects were still alive;
Bonaparte's chess set and games table,
the salon's centre pieces;
Richelieu's hangings and Flemish tapestries
draping the walls, the fireplace hooded
with stencilled limestone.

A girl looks away sadly into the distance
holding an orange meant to cheer her.
More self-aggrandizing portraits carry secrets,
ghosts already visiting before their lives are done.
They whisper in the music room, whisper
elegy and lyric over the mantelpiece

and the Albrecht Durer wood block,
over the Meissen Apostles whose frozen
puzzled looks speak discomfort in a world
denying modesty, humility, and self-control.
Ten thousand mostly unread books elongate
like bullet belts. Aurora in her chariot
thunders across the ceiling.

Ascend. Note the black-suited George,
aged eleven, seated at a table. Note
the smileless, confident face,
hands gently resting on thighs,
already a man, already schooled in severity and poise,
naturally imperial, his bedroom wrapped in purple
and gold silk fabrics. Paw-foot. Paw-foot.
Ascend...

Now descend to the blue marble downstairs,
corridor rock faces, severe as prison
walls, yet shanked in beauty,
cold marble that leads to a bowling
alley, guest recreation rooms,
a swimming pool, rotisserie kitchen, laundry
and drying rooms, canning and kitchen pantries,
and the servants' bedrooms where sexual indiscretions,
like those on plantations, were as common as the pox.

EARLY BIRDS

Pre-dawn darkness.
Mockingbirds, loud, happy,
fastened to the morning like grommets.
Two older women with cane lances
walk slowly in conversation.
A group of shirtless men
run and talk. A young woman jogs
alone and unafraid.

Two blossoming dogwoods
suddenly rise softly from a lawn
like Civil War ghosts guarding the red-brick columns
that are stitched with ivy sutures.
The moon's a half wafer on God's lips
over Arsenal and Walton Way, over
the earth-compacted dead.

Hooded and panting, I inhale
cool air as yet untarnished
by the day's exhausts. I move
with my own particular ease,
my own particular joy, alone
but not lonely, finding
some merited peace
in exile's daily course.

LOCK AND DAM

Where the dam breaks is creation's primal force.
Where the ringed copperhead gazes, a congruity with humans.
Where a water moccasin hangs is the vault of temptation.
Where geese rest by the break, the anvil of self-assurance.
Where the skink flashes is the wall of memory.
Where the shaved trunk poses is the art of the beaver.
Where bank and water meet is harmony's praise.
Where the sun emerges is an enemy's defeat.
Where it is covered, the heart's temporary defeat.
Where the tree's uprooted is the fate of empires.
Where rapid voices gather is the song of human need:
a city's quota of water, boat races, regattas,
anadromous fish passing upstream.

THE BLEACHING PROCESS

A faded ankle-length cotton dress;
a buttoned-down black long-sleeved sweater;
wiry hands raised in triumphant praise,
palms lightly quivering with gratitude
like allamanda petals in a breeze.
The scarfed head, with its wide, watery
bone-white irises, points upward,
lips rustling with thanks.

The coal-coloured face is gleaming.
Palm fronds, like her arms, spread outward
and rise from a spot behind her
in the yard near the back door
of the small stone house,
white paint chipping and peeling in spots,
a crack here and there.

Seated on a wooden chair next to her,
the shawled, brown-skinned daughter in white
pinafore-like dress points to
the matriarch and tells the child
on her lap, "*Aquela é a vovó*. That's Grandma."

The child, the colour of ivory, points
a responsive finger toward Grandma
while clutching an apple in the other hand.
Across the opened back door space, a high line
holds pieces of clothing that foreground a darkness
intensifying in the receding depths of a cave.

A man sits in the doorway,
his smirking face a scarf of self-satisfaction,
legs gently crossed, interlocked fingers
lightly clasping the upper knee,

the lower foot resting on random stone steps.
Sandals. Checkered pants. White Tee.
His eyes softly glow with love
at the straight hair on the child's head,
his white arms; with satisfaction
in the success of his genes; and with gladness
for the matriarch's approval of the plan.

PONTA NEGRA

Natal's eastern tip stretches like a tabby
toward Africa. Waves curl, hiss, and crash
with the same insistence as Bathsheba's
and with the same feral intent.
The Farol do Cabo Branco lighthouse stares
eternally into that distant origin,
its one lighted eye aching.

Once a garrison for U.S. troops,
now home to the Brazilian airforce,
its former ethnography ensured
an immense concentration of blue eyes
conceived to the throb of Forró music
(named after the star-striped sign
on the luring barracks – "Party For All" –
"Are you going to the For All?"
locals asked their friends on weekends).
Couples still shake and grind to the sensuous mix
of American country and native syncopations
with accordion, triangle, zabumba drum.

Encircling these sounds for miles,
dunes famously do their own shifting
dance. Sometimes they swallow summer houses,
loop as dangerously as one-sided love
or land-robbed Amerindians,
ruler and ruled complicit in the skill of dying.
Was the risk worth the thrill –
that ride on the edge of death,
the adventure of knowing your taste, your touch –
as we lay illicitly spooned in bed?
Ponta Negra's black rocks wail
with the same impassable sorrow

as those at Bathsheba and Cattlewash,
bodies barnacled, waists eroding.

My eyes leap inward to the concreteness of hills,
to tortured barefoot peasants
working land they'll never own,
then turn again to the water's dangerous embrace,
constant in its rage, my rage,
the rage of all those brought
to Natal, Bahia, Recife, Barbados,
against their will.

CAMPINA GRANDE

After the tense flight over Pernambuco,
we reach Paraíba state where fifty percent
earn less than fifty dollars a month
and subsidized housing projects get only token water,
or electricity. There's no money for repairs.
Cracked roofs of terracotta, thick with grime,
are blackened almost beyond recognition.

In the mall on a wooden bench, I catch
my breath, witness here, as elsewhere,
the middle-class buzz and groan
of swarming intent: to work, to belong,
play pinball machines, have lunch, keep the children busy
so they'll be less irritable during the summer break.
I hear the clang of cutlery, the gallop
of cash registers, the myriad concurrent conversations
united in rhythm and form.

Here walls circle middle and upper-class houses so high
that all you see behind them are the blackened roofs.
On top of these walls glint razor-sharp prongs,
rooted in cement like sharks' teeth. Their fluid fins
stir fear in upwards-squinting thieves.

All inhabit the same trembling space,
though in Georgia, high walls are not needed,
subjects having been conditioned
to keep a respectable bullet-avoiding distance.
In Barbados, though walls are only mid-height,
with broken glass bottles sprinkled on some,
blood-eyed dogs will greet you.

Why haven't they revolted? Why do they not revolt?
We sip the marvellous *São Braz* coffee. Ana says,
in both rebuke and earnest belief,
"Brazilians, we are a peaceful people."

JOÃO PESSOA

1

Two lined Jewish faces, grave and solemn
beneath black-banded fedoras;
bodies craned forward in that anxious way
of passengers on a bumpy flight, yet with a measure
of resolve or faith that clings to past certainties.
Dark suspender-gripped slacks and light-green shirts
move towards the plane's exit.
It's hard to tell the nationality of the two women with them,
but beside that male austerity, the women's green dresses
and loosely hanging bonnet strings
are the difference between freedom and stolidity.

No more seats in economy gains a free
upgrade to *Classe Executiva*. "Obrigado," I tell the
flight attendant, who returns with caramel sweets
in glittering wraps twisted at the ends
in a small straw basket. They remind me of the toffees
we relished as children which stuck to our teeth,
our reflexive tongues angling to dislodge
the sticky bits, the taste lingering long.
She comes again in her laid-back way
with heavily-salted peanuts, cashews, almonds.
My neighbour declines with a "Sem sal, obrigado".
It *is* visibly thick, but I take some anyway.

2

São Paulo rises with an ochre haze that stretches
the length of the visible horizon.
Through the terminal, surprisingly low on traffic
for the world's largest city of over twenty million,

a local voice sings Marley's "Three Little Birds",
with string arrangements and an alternative edge,
high-pitched and twanging like Chinese opera.
Deserted? But then how can the impoverished eighty percent,
landless peasants in clay houses with dirt floors,
no electricity, no sanitary facilities, afford a ticket on Tam?

Over here in Pernambuco's backlands
near Recife, João Pessoa, Natal, in Campina Grande
men consume only half the calories they need for work,
a diet of manioc flour and black beans,
occasional jerked beef; seventy percent illiterate
against the dismal national average of fifty.
Like Carolina, they trudge with their bundles
from the countryside to São Paulo and Rio,
hoping for work, food, shelter.
Like her, they settle in squalid *favelas*,
earnings a little better than in their villages,
but a lot less safe.

We enter Pernambuco's airspace and then Recife's.
Meadows and mountain-sides are capped
in deep, lush green, textured like the fine rug
on which Cabral gleefully walked, eyeing the natives
and rubbing prurient hands together,
gone quite mad at the vision of gold.
Today, some tourists still speak the same language,
minds running wild with their own golden dreams
of shops in malls or lining the streets near their hotels.
They walk through the people, thinking:
at three reais to the dollar, what wonders can be possessed!
Then, exhausted and empty still, they
long to feast their eyes on other things,
like the Iguaçu Falls further south,
or the *Carnaval* where the natives play mass,
the men's pectorals and deltoids pumping,

the women in sequined thongs,
little seashells stuck over their tits,
lithe, shining bodies gyrating to the samba…

The Recife coastline, aquamarine-spotted, muddies
for a distance, then grows Atlantic dark green.
Farther out, its coal-coloured hide expands
before reversing to earlier variegations
onto the mainland opposite: João Pessoa.

3

Coconut trees, fronded heads like the jacks
we tossed at onesies, nestled
in groves or between larger trunks,
peer at the carefully crafted clay-tile roofs.
In a dirt yard, six boys chase a soccer ball
their patterns outlining one escape
from poverty's arrowing ache. At the least,
discipline, exercise, identity; at the most, another Pelé,
Ronaldo. This and samba their only chance.

Across from the Igatu Praia Hotel, night falls on the beach
lit with young men playing *futebol*.
In a nearby restaurant, that easy slip
between poverty and extravagance:
plaintains, cassava, pea salad, artichoke-like head-of-palm,
huge, boiled shrimps; quail eggs, same taste as a chicken's
but the size of a marble; buffalo cheese with its soft delicate
aftertaste. An assortment of fresh-cooked, skewered meats
arrive in ten-minute intervals, THE GAÚCHOS
in dark slacks and white aprons holding
laminated cards with drawings of cow, pig and lamb,
slicing appropriate cuts onto a plate or, receiving a head-shake,
gliding to the next patron, ready to carve, to please.

4

I wake to the birds' choir, light slanting rain,
and the writhe of coconut, almond, casuarina.
The beach deserted now, brown and yellow plastic chairs
lean forward like penitents onto the circular beach tables.
This could be Brandon's Beach, Barbados.
A blonde man strides along the waterfront
(a Bajan woman jogs on a south coast pavement).
He's comfortable in white Tee and tennis shoes.
The rain cannot interrupt his preparation of mind and body
for another day at the office.

EVERY CAROLINA

1

I know your reluctant daily walk to the spigot –
my stand-pipe – teeming with jars, cans, gossip, crudeness.
There was more nastiness there than painted
in the sentimental notions of folk beauty,
of good-hearted stories told by earthy matriarchs. What
we heard cut like the raw edge of a tongue.
The middle-class do nothing but romanticize
our pain, expiate guilt over desertion or good luck.
I see you each morning in the lengthening line of hunger,
smell the human faeces smeared on the pipe stand.

I walked the length of my gap with paint skillets
to get water from the stand-pipe. I did my business
in an outhouse with brown-bag paper for wipes,
one skillet with me in the bathing area,
always fetid, home of millipedes and large oozing slugs.

Your honest, transparent heart, blooded by trial,
pumping the true salve of survival, speaks to me.
I follow you hitting the streets of Canindé, collecting
paper to sell at the junkyard to get a meal
for the children, or get them something to wear.
Some mornings, there's no food.
Some days, there's no paper.
You look for scrap metal, raid the tomato factory
for fruit spilled during off-loading.
Sometimes you sleep with one child's
father, so he'll give something – shoes, a dress,
some cruzeiros – when he comes, and sends the children
to buy candy so you can be together.
At times like these, you're disgusted to be a woman.
Your spirit flaps like a bird when he goes away.

Yet, you're a woman of your word,
keeping the promise not to mention
his name in your diaries,
or give it to the newspapers.
Sometimes you sleep with Mr. Manuel,
the most distinguished man here,
with a strong work ethic like your own,
never missing a day from work.
He, too, is generous when he has his way,
when you don't anger him by flirting
with emigrant men – the Baianos, the Gypsies.
You're in the favela, but you're not favela.
You're in the ghetto, but you're not ghetto.
You save your smiles for the children.

Your favela reaches northward to a pot-holed gap
just outside Bridgetown where a woman
borrows water from a neighbour 'cause hers was cut off,
a hose like a green snake writhing across the road
from the neighbour's yard.
The neighbour's sister speaks to no-one,
including her sister. She curses her children,
calls them idiot, fool, rasshole,
her children from several different men
with their empty promises of help,
children who no longer find unusual
the sight of a naked woman,
children immune to every vice.

You dreamed of getting away
from the paedophiles, of having
a nice home, escaping the scandalous spigot,
the smell of rotten mud mixed with faeces,
the fetid pools of bathwater in the mud tracks,
the animal-pen stench behind the shacks,
the curse of hunger, the curse of thieves.

2

Your words tell aches I've known, and seen in others
no matter what the class. Abuse by men,
self-appointed owners, gaolers, critics.
After five children, Mrs. Stoute's forgotten
in a domestic cell, while Mr. Stoute indulges
with four others. When she put her arms around him,
he says it doesn't suit her. The brick house she lives in
is the kind you always dreamed of owning:
potted plants in the porch, a room for each child.

While my poverty was mild compared
to the lines of shacks on São Paulo's hillsides,
my neighbourhood a fraction the size of Canindé,
there are echoes that penetrate the barrier of language,
as your words put flesh on the dream of freedom.
While the world toasted the success of your Diary,
Brazil's foppish literati (culture managers, academics,
middle-class writers) ignored you, found ways
to pull you down. Twenty-six years after your body
became a dry branch and your spirit soared heavenward
after a pauper's burial at Vila Cipó, I hear your voice
husky and strong like a blues singer's.
The South's deciduous kudzu and the island's
perennial love-vines coil and loop
in a lovely, dangerous embrace.
I see your arms in flight like a cobbler's wings
pumping implacably over my coast in search of food,
refusing to die, refusing to be silenced.

GLOSSARY

"The Migration", p. 12: In 2004, a big controversy erupted between Barbados and Trinidad and Tobago over the alleged migration of Barbadian flying fish into Trinidad and Tobago's territorial waters. Many Barbadian fishermen were apprehended by Trinidadian authorities and had their catches confiscated.

Silver men: the name given to West Indian labourers who worked on the construction of the Panama Railroad in the 1850s and the Panama Canal between 1881 and 1914.

"The *Henrietta Marie*", pp. 13-14, was a slave ship that sank around 1700 on New Ground Reef near Key West, Florida, on its return journey to England.

Kneller: Godfrey Kneller, seventeenth-century German-born English painter.

"Three Beaches", p. 15: "Philip, My Dear" was a 1983 song by calypsonian, The Mighty Sparrow.

"Nature as Shrink", p. 18: Iona Potopov was the main protagonist in Chekov's short story, "Misery".

"Tuk Haikus", p. 20: Bing Crosby, Rosemary Clooney, Danny Kaye and Vera-Ellen were stars of the 1954 movie, *White Christmas*.

"Caliban", p. 25: Whitman, Walt. "This Compost", *Leaves of Grass*. New York and Scarborough: New American Library, Signet Classic, 1980. 293-294.

Sobers: Barbadian Sir Garfield Sobers, arguably the world's greatest all-round cricket player, is officially and erroneously spoken of in Barbados as the island's only living legend.

"Tale of the Yard Fowls", p. 26: *Tuk Verse*: the author's verse invention derived from vocal melodies and drum patterns of Barbados's indigenous folk music called Tuk.

Anancy: Caribbean equivalent of Ananse, the West African spider god of tricks and stratagems

"*The Masters (Part Two)*", p. 39: *in Hootie Johnson's "[N]ot at the point of a bayonet"* quotes the former Chairman of the Augusta National Golf Club's response to feminist Martha Burk's challenge of the club's all-male membership.

"Biltmore", p. 41: Biltmore is the grandiose estate built by George Vanderbilt II in North Carolina.
nearing the end of a century: construction on the house started in 1889 and was completed in 1895;
Cornelia's marriage…: George's daughter married the British aristocrat, John F. A. Cecil in 1924, who took over the property when her mother, Edith, died in 1958. The Cecil family opened the house to the public in 1930.
Bonaparte: Napoleon Bonaparte.
Richelieu: Cardinal Richelieu, Seventeenth century French statesman.
A girl looks sadly away…: refers to the Renoir painting, "Girl With An Orange", one of two Renoirs at Biltmore. The other is "Young Algerian Girl."
Aurora in her chariot…: Eighteenth century Pellegrini painting.
…the black-suited George…: George Vanderbilt (1862-1914).

"Lock and Dam", p. 44: Savannah Bluff Lock and Dam in North Augusta, Georgia.
Skink: a common American lizard.

"The Bleaching Process", pp. 45-46: This poem is based on the 1895 painting by the Brazilian artist Modesto Brocos y Gomez (1852-1936) whose painting, *Redemption of Cam*, reveals the official racial attitudes in Brazil: "white blood" would bleach "black blood" to create a Europeanized Brazilian. In the painting, three generations – black grandmother, brown-skinned mother, and white child – portray the bleaching process.

"Ponta Negra", pp. 47-48: *Bathsheba…Cattlewash….:* neighbour-hoods along Barbados's wild Atlantic east coast.

Once a garrison for U.S. troops: During WWII.

"João Pessoa", pp. 51-54: *Carolina…*: Brazilian author Carolina Maria de Jesus (1914-1977)

Cabral: Portuguese explorer and nobleman, Pedro Alvares Cabral (1467-1520) who, on April 22, 1500, became the first European to see Brazil.

Bajan: vernacular for Barbadian, a citizen of Barbados.

"Every Carolina", pp. 55-58: Carolina Maria de Jesus (1914-1977) lived in a São Paulo favela or shanty slum. Black, illegitimate and poor, she became Brazil's best-selling author at the age of forty-six with the publication of her diaries, *Quarto de Despejo* (*The Garbage Room*).

Rasshole: Barbadian vernacular curse word.

Cobbler's wings…, p. 51: Eastern Caribbean name for the frigate or man-o'-war bird.

ABOUT THE AUTHOR

Anthony Kellman was born in Barbados in 1955, educated at Combermere School, at UWI (Cave Hill) and in the U.S. At eighteen he left for Britain where he worked as a troubadour playing pop and West Indian folk music on the pub and folk club circuit. During the 1980s he returned to Barbados where he worked as a newspaper reporter, then did a BA in English and History. Afterwards he worked in PR for the Central Bank of Barbados, experiences which he drew on in writing *The Coral Rooms*.

At this time he published two poetry chapbooks, *In Depths of Burning Lights* (1982) and *The Broken Sun* (1984), which drew praise from Kamau Brathwaite, among others.

In 1987 he left Barbados for the USA where he studied for a Masters of Fine Arts degree in Creative Writing at Lousiana State University. After completing in 1989 he moved to Augusta State University, Georgia, where he is Professor of Creative Writing.

In 1990 Peepal Tree published his third book of poetry, *Watercourse*, (which appeared with a glowing endorsement from Edouard Glissant), the novel, *The Coral Rooms* (1994), *The Long Gap* (1996) and *Wings of a Stranger* (2000). In 2004 came his second novel, *The Houses of Alphonso*, followed by *Limestone* (2008), his epic of Barbadian history written in Tuk verse forms. All his work has a powerful involvement with landscape, both as a living entity shaping peoples' lives and as a source of metaphor for inner processes. The limestone caves of Barbados have provided a particularly fertile source of inspiration.

ALSO BY ANTHONY KELLMAN

The Coral Rooms
ISBN: 9780948833533; pp. 102, pub. 1994; price: £6.95

Percival Veer has risen to the tenth floor of the Federal Bank of Charouga, has acquired a large and imposing house and a young and attentive wife. But satisfaction eludes him. Guilt over a past wrong begins to trouble him and a recurrent dream of caves disturbs his sleep. As Percy's inner world crumbles, he is gripped by an obsessive desire to explore the deep limestone caves of his island, dimly remembered from his boyhood. This gripping, poetic novel charts Percy's meeting with his spiritual guide, Cane Arrow, and his hallucinatory descent into the cave's depths.

'Realistic and dreamlike, explicit and mysterious... The descriptions are evocative & sensual. A compelling read.' – Carole Klein.

'A realistic and convincing portrait of self-loathing' – Wilson Harris.

The Houses of Alphonso
ISBN: 9781900715829; pp. 192, pub. 2004; price: £8.99

Barbadian-born Alphonso Hutson has lived in the USA for nearly sixteen years. But he cannot settle. He has dragged his long-suffering American wife, Simone, and their children from house to rented house. He has refused to share with her any real explanation for the complex feelings that drive him. But this time she has had enough of his 'sorry restlessness', refuses to move with him and threatens the end of their marriage. Only then is Alphonso forced into confronting the ghosts that propel his perpetual migrancy.

The ghosts lie in his native Barbados. There is the love, shame and guilt he feels for the dead parents whose funerals he failed to attend, and there is the mystery of the brother he has never seen, hidden away in an institution. All is complicated by his mixed feelings for his homeland. It is the place that still feeds his imagination, but as a boy from a Black working class family he has felt excluded from the class structures of a country still dominated by a privileged White minority.

Kellman combines a poetic exploration of Alphonso's personal journey into his past, with an acute engagement with racial and political issues of a country in the midst of turmoil as the old order is challenged.

Watercourse
ISBN: 9780948833373; pp. 64; pub. 1990; price: £5.99

The celebrated Martiniquan poet and novelist Edouard Glissant writes: '*Watercourse* is more than a collection of poems. It is the continual amazement evoked by Caribbean landscape: a single dialogue between the sea and the land... a song whose dazzling waves foam among the islands... Anthony Kellman's poetry has the strength and sweetness of vegetation with the power of progressively revealing to us the nature of the earth in which it grows.'

The Long Gap
ISBN: 9780948833786; pp. 64; pub. 1996; price: £6.99

The Long Gap is a passionate exploration of the Caribbean exile's need 'to go back/to clutch the roots of the word'. Writing out of the the fear of the 'gap' which can grow too long, Kellman engages with his Barbadian heritage as one which both sustains and drives to anger. In language which echoes the rhythms of the 'tuk' band and the 'scat of the guitar strum', he celebrates the traditions of resistance and creative invention, but excoriates the islands of cocaine, political corruption and subservience to external masters.

Bruce King writes: 'Tony Kellman is always trying something different... He is a serious poet and the various contradictions and affiliations found in his verse embody those of the Caribbean and, to generalise, most poetry. A formalist attracted towards, oral, folk and popular traditions, he also mixes the highly lyrical with dialect and the prose-like. I especially like his metaphors and patterns of sound. When reading these poems you feel that... here is one of our best younger poets.'

Wings of a Stranger
ISBN: 9781900715447; pp. 71; pub. 2000; price: £7.99

In the continuing rite of return to his native Barbados from longer and longer away, something has happened for Tony Kellman. No longer are these the alienated poems of *the long gap*, of belonging nowhere. With greater establishment in America has come, *on the wings of a stranger*, the capacity to embrace this past and to see wholly afresh what was once familiar and unremarked. Parallel to these poems of place, are those that explore new love and its power to heal.

As well as Barbados, there are poems set in worlds as different as sharecropping Georgia and Yorkshire, England. In all of them one hears Kellman's signal voice which combines his urbane capacity to 'hum forever simple pleasure' and the ecstatic vision of a poet who 'puts on the garment of praise' to 'retell our special story'.

Limestone
ISBN: 9781845230036; pp. 200; pub. 2008; price: £9.99

Limestone is the epic poem of Barbados and a major development in an indigenous Caribbean poetics. Drawing on the folk music of Tuk, Anthony Kellman invents his own forms of Tuk verse to write the story of his island from the destruction of the Amerindians to the present day.

Part one uses both invented characters and actual historical persons such as Bussa and Nanny Grigg, the leaders of the 1816 slave revolt, to explore the epic of loss, survival and reinvention in the lives of the African slaves. Part two is set in the post-emancipation period up to the twenty-first year of independence. Through the voices of those who led the struggle against colonialism – Samuel Jackman Prescod, Charles O'Neal, Clement Payne, Grantley Adams and Errol Barrow – Kellman explores their inner anguish over the slow pace of advance and the inevitable compromises with external power. And as the queues of would-be emigrants at the American consulate lengthen, the island asks: when a White business class still dominates the economy, who has benefited from the people's struggles of the past?

Part three is set at the end of the twentieth century and tells the stories of Livingston, a young musician, and Levinia, an Indian-African Barbadian schoolteacher who has migrated to the USA.

Limestone constructs a vision of Barbados that encompasses suffering and achievement, heroic struggle and the setbacks of born of self-interest and timorous compromise. Above all, *Limestone* is never other than a poem: a vast treasure house of images, sounds and rhythms that move, entertain and absorb the reader in its world.

All Peepal Tree titles are available from the website
www.peepaltreepress.com
with a money back guarantee, secure credit card ordering
and fast delivery throughout the world at cost or less.